BUDD

LITTLE BOOK OF LIFE

BUDDHAS'

LITTLE BOOK

OF LIFE

Daily Wisdom from the Great Masters,
Teachers, and Writers of All Time

MARK ZOCCHI

HAMPTON ROADS

Cover design by Jim Warner
Cover photograph © Steve Vidler / Superstock
Illustrations by Mark Zocchi
Interior by Kathryn Sky-Peck
Typeset in Weiss

Hampton Roads Publishing Company, Inc.
Charlottesville, VA 22906
Distributed by Red Wheel/Weiser, LLC
www.redwheelweiser.com
Sign up for our newsletter and special offers by going to
www.redwheelweiser.com/newsletter.

ISBN: 978-1-57174-799-0
Library of Congress Control Number: 2017952871

Printed in Canada
MAR

10 9 8 7 6 5 4 3 2 1

INTRODUCTION

Inspired by teachings of the Buddha, Great Masters, teachers, and writers, this book is designed to help people connect to a spiritual path and find their own divinity.

It is overflowing with wonderful quotes, sayings, and insights, each presented alone, allowing the reader to dip in at any time. Each reading is guaranteed to inspire either immediately or to provide food for thought.

Buddha means "the Awakened One" and sayings have been selected from the Buddha, who was Siddhartha before his enlightenment and Gautama Buddha, or Shakyamuni Buddha, after his enlightenment some 2,500 years ago.

Additional quotes and sayings have been chosen from other "Buddhas," masters of spirituality and inspiration, such as Padmasambhava, Milarepa, Shantideva, Nyoshul Khenpo Rinpoche, Dudjom Rinpoche, and Longchenpa. To their timeless wisdom has been added the philosophies of current-day Masters such as His Holiness the 14th Dalai Lama, Thich Nhat Hanh, and Sogyal Rinpoche.

Great Masters, teachers, and writers are found throughout humanity and from many diverse traditions. Words of wisdom and peace from Zen Master Roshi, Chuang Tzu, Cicero, Sufi poet Rumi, Lao Tzu, Mother Teresa, Thomas Merton, and William Shakespeare are also presented as part of this collection.

Buddhist tradition holds that all of us have our own Buddha nature but have not yet realized it, although each of us has glimpses into our true nature.

It is my wish that this book, inspired by these Masters, will encourage you to seek truth, peace, and wisdom in all you do.

MARK ZOCCHI

WORDS OF WISDOM

Of what avail is it if we can travel to the moon,
If we cannot cross the abyss that separates us from
ourselves,
This is the most important of all journeys
And without it all of the rest are useless.

THOMAS MERTON

Always connected
In my heart
No need to grasp
Smile with warm Heart

MARK ZOCCHI

We accept the graceful falling
Of mountain cherry blossoms,
But it is much harder for us
To fall away from our own
Attachment to the world.

ZEN

Simplicity, Patience, and Compassion

These three are your greatest treasures.

Simple in actions and in thought,

You return to the source of being.

Patience with both friends and enemies,

You accord with the way things are.

Compassionate toward yourself,

You reconcile all beings in the world.

TAO TE CHING

When my house burned down
I gained
An unobstructed view
of the moonlight sky

ZEN (RENUNCIATION/LETTING GO)

We find simplicity in our hearts and lives through paying attention to the roots of our complexity and letting go.

CHRISTINA FELDMAN

Out of clutter,
find simplicity.
From discord,
find harmony.
In the middle of difficulty
lies opportunity.

ALBERT EINSTEIN

In the pursuit of Knowledge,
every day something is gained.
In the pursuit of freedom,
every day something is let go.

TAO

To abandon what is harmful,
To adopt what is wholesome,
To purify the heart and mind:
This is the teaching of the Buddha.

BUDDHA

Before enlightenment, all things in the outer world are deceptive and confusing. After enlightenment, we see all things as magic shadow-plays, and all objective things become helpful friends.

MILAREPA

13

To free oneself of knowledge is to die, and thus one lives.

KRISHNAMURTI

Desire, anger and delusion are negative forces,
but they also represent the energy and majesty
of the Buddha-nature in its elemental state.
The practice of Buddhism is concerned with becoming
aware of these passions and calming them
until they are transformed into joy, warmth,
generosity, energy and wisdom.
Once familiar with these forces,
we can work with and transform them.

HIS HOLINESS THE 14TH DALAI LAMA

If you see the soul in every living being,
you see truly.
If you see immortality in the heart of
every mortal being, you see truly.

THE BHAGAVAD GITA

What is the soul?

The soul is consciousness.

It shines as the light within the heart.

BRIHADARANYAKA UPANISHAD

There are thousands of lives in one single life.

SVAMI PRAJNANPAD

We may idealize freedom, but when it comes to our habits, we are completely enslaved.

SOGYAL RINPOCHE

The mind is like a fertile field—
all sorts of things can grow there.
When we plant a seed—an act, a statement, or a
thought—it will eventually produce a fruit,
which will ripen and fall to the ground
and perpetuate more of the same. Moment by
moment, we plant potent seeds of causation with our
body, speech, and mind. When the right conditions
come together for our karma to ripen, we will have to
deal with the consequences of what we have planted.

CHAGDUD TULKU RINPOCHE

The nature of everything is illusory and ephemeral.
Those with dualistic perception regard suffering
as happiness; they are like those who lick honey
from a razor's edge.
How pitiful are they who cling to concrete reality;
turn your attention within, my friends.

NYOSHUL KHENPO RINPOCHE

A man who has had his way is seldom happy,
for generally he finds that the way does not lead
very far on this earth of desires
which can never be fully satisfied.

JOSEPH CONRAD

Although we are responsible for what we sow, we forget that we've planted these seeds and either give credit to or blame people or things outside of us when they ripen. . . . In the moment, we have a thought, we speak or act. But we lose sight of the fact that each thought, word, and action will produce a result. When the fruit finally ripens, we think, "Why did this happen to me? I've done nothing to deserve this."

CHAGDUD TULKU RINPOCHE

Does a flower, full of beauty, light and loveliness say,
"I am giving, helping, serving?"
It is! And because it is not trying to do anything
it covers the earth.

KRISHNAMURTI

He who is tolerant like the earth,
firm as a pillar and clear as a
mountain pool, such a man will never
be reborn.

THE DHAMMAPADA

Without faith man can do nothing:
with it all things are possible.

SIR WILLIAM OSLER

By ourselves evil is done;

by ourselves we suffer.

By ourselves evil is left undone;

by ourselves we are purified.

Purity and impurity are personal concerns.

No one person

can purify another.

THE DHAMMAPADA

It is vitally important to remember that no matter
what stage of meditation we are engaged with,
we should, at all times, fully
appreciate and respect our practice.

THE DZOGCHEN PONLOP RINPOCHE

The happiness that we desire and the suffering that we shun come about as a result of causes and conditions. Understanding this causal mechanism of suffering and happiness is what the Four Noble Truths are all about.

HIS HOLINESS THE 14TH DALAI LAMA

Right understanding means to understand things
as they really are and not as they appear to be.
It is self-examination and self observation.

PIYADASSI THERA

Man falls from the pursuit of the ideal of plain living and high thinking the moment he wants to multiply his daily wants. Man's happiness really lies in contentment.

MAHATMA GANDHI

The practice of meditation takes us on a journey that is very personal and very lonely. Only the individual knows what he or she is doing, and it is a very lonely journey. However, if one were doing it alone without any reference to the lineage, without any reference to the teacher and the teachings, it would not be lonely, because you would have a sense of being involved in the process of developing the self-made man. So you would feel less lonely. You would feel like you were on the way to becoming a hero. It is particularly because of the commitment that one makes to the teachings and the lineage and the teacher that the meditative journey becomes such a lonely one.

CHÖGYAM TRUNGPA RINPOCHE

If I give all I possess to the poor and surrender my body to the flames but have not love, I gain nothing.

CORINTHIANS

Thus you shall think of all this fleeting world:
a bubble in a stream,
a flash of lightning in a summer cloud,
a flickering lamp, a phantom,
and a dream.

THE DIAMOND SUTRA

The basic purpose, or the basic development that we are making in meditation practice is to develop more mindfulness and awareness and to gain, or to discover—to rediscover, so to speak—our basic wisdom to transcend our emotions. The reason we say "rediscover" here is that this wisdom to transcend our emotions is already there. It already exists as part of our mind, as a nature of our mind; it's not something new that we are learning from this spiritual journey. Therefore, in this meditation practice, on this meditation path, we are trying to develop the ultimate realization through developing greater mindfulness and awareness. We are trying to familiarize ourselves more closely with the basic nature of our mind so that we can realize the ultimate nature of our mind.

THE DZOGCHEN PONLOP RINPOCHE

To know our soul apart from our ego is the first step toward accomplishing the supreme deliverance. It is necessary that we know with absolute certainty that in essence we are spirit. And we can only arrive at this knowledge if we render ourselves masters of our ego, if we rise above all pride, all appetite, all fear, by knowing that material losses and the death of the body can never take away the truth and the greatness of our soul.

RABINDRANATH TAGORE

There is no weapon more powerful in
achieving the truth than
acceptance of oneself.

SVAMI PRAJNANPAD

Death is extraordinarily like life,
when we know how to live.
You cannot live without dying.
You cannot live if you do not die
psychologically every minute.

KRISHNAMURTI

The name given to the Buddhist teachings is Dharma in Sanskrit and Dhamma in Pali (an ancient Indian language). Dharma or Dhamma encompasses not only the teachings but also the universal law that is inherent in all things and informs all things. With a small "d," dharma and dhamma mean the smallest elements of existence that make up a moment of consciousness, such as the heat of a room, background sounds, the lingering taste of the orange you have just eaten, the smell of incense, the thoughts you have. All these scraps of information are dharmas or dhammas. They are in a continuous pulse of movement, of coming to be and ceasing to be; nevertheless, we experience them as continuous reality.

THE DHAMMAPADA

If you are in the moment, you are in the infinite.

SVAMI PRAJNANPAD

The nature of your mind, which cannot be
pinpointed, is innate and original wakefulness.
It is important to look into yourself
and recognize your nature.

PADMASAMBHAVA

It is important to become familiar with meditation. Once we've become familiar with it, we can use it however we want. To understand this more clearly, let's look at the word for meditation in Tibetan. In English, although we have different words for it, usually we simply use the word meditation.

In Tibetan, the word is Gom, which means "getting accustomed to," "getting used to," "getting familiar with." When we meditate, we're becoming familiar with something. What we're getting used to is the view of the meditation practice we're doing. As we get more and more used to it, the level of profundity deepens. The meditation penetrates deeper and deeper. This applies to all the different kinds of meditation we do.

SAKYONG MIPHAM RINPOCHE

There is no master, there is no instructor,
there is no person to tell you what you must do.

KRISHNAMURTI

Sometimes when we see too much truth about ourselves suddenly mirrored by the teacher or the teachings, it is simply too difficult to face, too terrifying to recognize, too painful to accept as the reality. And when there are things too difficult to accept about ourselves, we project them, usually onto those who love us and help us the most—our teacher, the teachings, our parent or our closest friend.

SOGYAL RINPOCHE

Those who are focused on the objects of the senses, become attached to those objects. From attachment comes desire; and from desire comes anger; from anger comes confusion of mind; from confusion of mind comes loss of memory; from loss of memory comes loss of intelligence; and from loss of intelligence comes destruction.

THE BHAGAVAD GITA

Good friends, my teaching of the Dharma takes
meditation and wisdom as its basis.
Never under any circumstances say that
meditation and wisdom are different.
They are one unity, not two things.
Meditation itself is the substance of wisdom, and
wisdom itself is the substance of meditation.

HUINENG

We must refuse to be lifted off our feet.

A drowning man cannot save others.

MAHATMA GANDHI

When you walk, just walk. When you sit, just sit.
Just be your ordinary, natural self in ordinary life,
unconcerned in seeking for Buddhahood. When
you're tired, lie down. The fool will laugh at you but
the wise man will understand.

LIN-CHI

The one thing common to all mediation practice is
having the right motivation of wanting to benefit
all persons, not just ourselves. Besides this, we also
need to have very strong devotion to our guru and
all the gurus of our lineage. If we pray to them with
really sincere devotion, we can receive their blessings,
which lead to a very rapid growth of our meditation.

KHENCHEN THRANGU RINPOCHE

There is a transcendent power in example.
We reform others unconsciously when we walk
uprightly.

ANNE SOPHIE SWETCHINE

Earth brings us to life and nourishes us.

Earth takes us back again.

Birth and death are present in every moment.

THICH NHAT HANH

To be rich in admiration and free from envy, to rejoice greatly in the good of others, to love with such generosity of heart that your love is still a dear possession in absence or unkindness

—these are gifts which money cannot buy.

ROBERT LOUIS STEVENSON

When the soil of trust that is a pure mind is soaked by the rain of merit, the sprouts of the wholesome and healthy in the world grow large and the crop of excellence of the Victorious One ripens.

LONGCHENPA

They are learned and compassionate, their profound intelligence and their spiritual horizon is like the sky. In their kindness they are never lazy but always diligent. And they apply themselves to raising mankind.

LONGCHENPA

Something to do.
Someone to love and
Something to hope for.

INDIAN PROVERB

Instead of really practicing dharma, we often only talk about practicing dharma. The more we talk without practicing, the more we lose our energy in words and so the more our point of view is lost.

THINLEY NORBU RINPOCHE

Do not believe a thing simply because it has been said.

Do not put your faith in traditions only because they have been honored by many generations.

Do not believe a thing because the general opinion believes it to be true or because it has been said repeatedly.

Do not believe a thing because of the single witness of one of the sages of antiquity.

Do not believe a thing because the probabilities are in its favor, or because you are in the habit of believing it to be true.

Do not believe in that which comes to your imagination, thinking that it must be the revelation of a superior Being.

Believe nothing that binds you to the sole authority of your masters or priests.

That which you have tried yourself, which you have experienced, which you have recognized as true, and which will be beneficial to you and to others; believe that and shape your conduct to it.

BUDDHA

When we begin to practice the
basic meditation of tranquillity meditation
[shamatha], we may find that our mind won't stay still
for a moment. But this condition is not permanent
and will change as we practice. Eventually we will
be able to place our mind at rest at will, at which
point we will have successfully alleviated the
manifest disturbance of the disturbing emotions.
After developing tranquillity meditation, we can then
apply the second technique, of insight meditation
[vipashyana], which consists of learning to recognize
and directly experience the nature of our own mind.
This nature is referred to as emptiness. When we
recognize this nature, and rest in it, then all of the
disturbing emotions that arise dissolve into this
emptiness and are no longer afflictions. This is the
freedom, which is called Buddhahood.

KHENCHEN THRANGU RINPOCHE

The most important aspect is to cultivate a good motivation and to carry out your daily program within it. Early in the morning as well as late in the night, you can spend at least half an hour in practice—meditation, recitation, daily yoga, or the like. Then, while working during the day, you should remember the motivation.

HIS HOLINESS THE 14TH DALAI LAMA

It is good to have an end to journey towards; but it is the journey that matters in the end.

URSULA K. LE GUIN

What are the characteristics of worthy people? Their bodily presence inspires calmness and their actions are pure and faultless. They are wise in dispelling doubts and their words are pleasant and clear. Their mind is very calm and a veritable treasure of omniscience.

LONGCHENPA

Think about death and impermanence
for a long time. Once you are certain
that you are going to die,
you will no longer find it hard to put aside
harmful actions nor difficult to do what is right.
After that, meditate for a long time on love and
compassion. Once love fills your heart
you will no longer find it hard to dispel all your
delusions. Then meditate for a long time
on emptiness, the natural state. Once you fully
understand emptiness, you will no longer
find it hard to dispel all your delusions.

GESHE POTOWA

Every time you smile at someone,
it is an action of love,
a gift to that person,
a beautiful thing.

MOTHER TERESA

Whoever wishes to quickly become a refuge for himself and others should undertake this sacred mystery: to take the place of others, giving them his own.

SHANTIDEVA

When the heart weeps for what it has lost,
the spirit laughs for what it has found.

SUFI PROVERB

Reality is that which, when you stop believing in it,
doesn't go away.

PHILIP K DICK

By selfless giving, by being generous, we cease to be niggardly and become liberal not only with our wealth but with our thoughts.

PIYADASSI THERA

Having meditated on love and compassion, I forgot the difference between myself and others.

Having meditated on my lama, I forgot those who are influential and powerful.

Having meditated on yidam,

I forgot the coarse world of the senses.

Having meditated on the instruction of the secret tradition, I forgot the books of dialectic.

Having tasted the joys of solitude, I forgot the need to please my relatives and friends.

Having assimilated the teaching in my stream of consciousness, I forgot to engage in doctrinal polemics.

Having lived in humility in body and mind, I forgot the disdain and arrogance of the great.

Having made a monastery within my body, I forgot the monastery outside. Having embraced the spirit rather than the letter, I forgot how to play with words.

MILAREPA

To mourn too long for those we love is self-indulgent

But to honor their memory with a promise

To live a little better for having known them

Gives purpose to their life and an easier acceptance of
their death.

No one ever grew poor through giving alms.

ITALIAN PROVERB

What a wonderful life I've had!
I only wish I'd realized it sooner.

COLETTE

If beings knew, as I know, the results of sharing gifts, they would not enjoy their gifts without sharing them with others, nor would the taint of stinginess obsess the heart and stay there. Even if it were their very last bit of food, they would not enjoy its use without sharing it if there were anyone to receive it.

BUDDHA

We have a confused society, in which everybody struggles to protect himself or herself, and where genuine, basic kindness itself seems so very difficult. But if we sit down and think about it, compassion and kindness aren't something that we have to learn from someone else. Kindness is the intrinsic nature; it is an intrinsic feeling that we all appreciate, and one really doesn't need especially to meditate or practice how to be a good person, how to refrain from harming another person, or to realize that killing, stealing, lying, and so on are negative. All of us [already] understand that.

KHANDRO RINPOCHE

Love is the only thing we carry with us when we go, and it makes the end so easy.

LOUISA MAY ALCOTT

I am unable to restrain external things,

but I shall restrain my own mind.

What need is there to restrain anything else?

SHANTIDEVA

We are all born for love. It is the principle of existence, and its only end.

DISRAELI

Sitting quietly, doing nothing
Spring comes and the grass grows by itself.

TAOIST POEM

Within you is a stillness and a sanctuary to which you can retreat at any time and be yourself.

HERMAN HESSE, *SIDDHARTHA*

The ideals which have lighted my way, and time after time have given me new courage to face life cheerfully, have been kindness, beauty, and truth.

ALBERT EINSTEIN

It is easy to do what is harmful to ourselves.
What is helpful and good is hard to do.

THE DHAMMAPADA

We can be as free of regret from failure by being
restored to virtue as by never having sinned.
A person who sees his faults and
confesses them will be pure.

ATISA

Inner tranquillity comes from the development of love and compassion. The more we care for the happiness of others, the greater is our own sense of well-being. Cultivating a close, warmhearted feeling for others automatically puts the mind at ease and opens the inner door.

HIS HOLINESS THE 14TH DALAI LAMA

It is not only what we do,
but also what we do not do,
for which we are accountable.

MOLIÈRE

Moral excellence comes about as a result of habit. We become just by doing just acts, temperate by doing temperate acts, and brave by doing brave acts.

ARISTOTLE

An evil man may wish to injure the Virtuous One and, raising his head, spit toward heaven, but the spit, far from reaching heaven, will return and descend upon himself. Virtue cannot be destroyed, while evil inevitably destroys itself.

BUDDHA

Seek not good from without; seek it within yourselves, or you will never find it.

EPICTETUS

If we are truly in the present moment, and are not being carried away by our thoughts and fantasies, then we are in a position to be free of fate and available to our destiny.

RESHAD FEILD

Pain in life is inevitable, but misery is optional.

HENRY WARD BEECHER

It seems to me that the greatest stumbling block in life is this constant struggle to reach, to achieve, to acquire.

KRISHNAMURTI

Compassion is the key to the open way, the Mahayana, makes possible the transcendental actions of the bodhisattva. The bodhisattva path starts with generosity and openness—giving and openness. . . . The main theme of the open way is that we must begin to abandon the basic struggle of ego.
To be completely open, to have that kind of trust in yourself is the real meaning of compassion and love.

CHÖGYAM TRUNGPA RINPOCHE

If we truly desire to be happy, there is no other way to proceed but by the way of virtue: it is the method by which happiness is achieved.

HIS HOLINESS THE 14TH DALAI LAMA

When we, as individuals, first rediscover our spirit, we are usually drawn to nurture and cultivate this awareness.

SHAKTI GAWAIN

Have few desires and be content, because desires
produce dissatisfaction.

LONGCHENPA

My whole life, in one sense, has been an experiment in how to be a portable sanctuary—learning to practice the presence of God in the midst of stresses and strains for contemporary life.

RICHARD J. FOSTER

We have to understand the incredible suffering
that exists in the world.
If we do not understand suffering,
we are not really relating to the situation.
Most of us do not relate to the suffering;
we ignore the basic nature of what is going on.
When we contemplate the pain that there is,
we do relate to it. We understand the incredible
depths of the sorrow and misery that sentient beings
are going through, tormented and tormenting
themselves endlessly. We realize that this does
not need to happen, and we find a tremendous
compassion arising within us.

SAKYONG MIPHAM RINPOCHE

Only those who know when enough is enough can ever have enough.

LAO TZU

What the superior person seeks is in himself; what the smaller person seeks is in others.

CONFUCIUS

The person who has subdued the mind and senses and who is free from desires, attains freedom and karma through renunciation.

THE BHAGAVAD GITA

Knowing others is wisdom.

Knowing yourself is superior wisdom.

LAO TZU

You don't have to reform yourself
or abandon yourself,
but work with yourself.
That your passion, aggression, ignorance,
and everything is workable,
part of the path.

CHÖGYAM TRUNGPA RINPOCHE

We do not receive wisdom, we must discover it for ourselves, after a journey through the wilderness which no one else can make for us, which no one can spare us, for our wisdom is the point of view from which we come at last to regard the world.

MARCEL PROUST

Serenity is an inner peace that is present even in difficult surroundings.

WILLIAM V. PIETSCH

Better one day of wise and thoughtful life than one hundred years of folly and thoughtlessness.

THE DHAMMAPADA

Those who know don't lecture;
those who lecture don't know.

LAO TZU

Since you are like no other being
ever created since the beginning of time,
you are incomparable.

BRENDA UELAND

People are like stained-glass windows.
They sparkle and shine when the sun is out,
but when the darkness sets in
their true beauty is revealed only
if there is light from within.

ELISABETH KÜBLER-ROSS

Usually the concept of compassion or love is something like closeness or a feeling toward your friend. And also, sometimes, compassion means a feeling of pity—that is wrong. Compassion, or love in which someone looks down on another—that's not genuine compassion. Genuine compassion must be acting on the basis of respect and the realization or recognition that others also, just like myself, have the right to be happy.

HIS HOLINESS THE 14TH DALAI LAMA

The wise walk on, clinging to nothing.
They are neither elated by happiness
nor cast down by sorrow.

THE DHAMMAPADA

Thus at the centre of the self
there is a hole and a mystery.
Our own soul is unknown to us.

THOMAS AQUINAS

When we talk about compassion, love, and kindness, we are not talking about a kind of "sacred heart" or external grace that we are trying to extend to someone who is suffering. When we talk about compassion here, we are talking about the fundamental state of compassion, the fundamental state of our heart, which goes beyond the conceptual idea of being compassionate. Therefore, the acts of bodhisattva are spontaneous acts of compassion, which are not fabricated. These acts are not based on concepts or preconceived notions of how or what they should be. They are spontaneous, natural, on-the-spot experiences of this heart. For that reason, many sutras give the example of a mother's compassion to express this experience.

When a mother sees her only child suffering, the spontaneous heart of compassion arises without any preconceptions or preparation. A mother does not have to prepare her compassion; when she sees her child, it is right there.

The bodhisattva heart of compassion is very spontaneous and on the spot. It goes beyond any conceptual reality, any idea of formulating love or compassion.

THE DZOGCHEN PONLOP RINPOCHE

If you understand others, you are astute.
If you understand yourself,
you are insightful.

LAO TZU

There is nothing on earth so curious for beauty
or so absorbent of it as a soul.

WASSILY KANDINSKY

The wise man guards his mind, which is unruly and ever in search of pleasure. The mind well-guarded brings great happiness.

THE DHAMMAPADA

He who understands the true nature of life is the happiest individual, for he is not upset by the fleeting nature of things. He tries to see things as they are, and not as they seem to be.

PIYADASSI THERA

To laugh often and love much,

To win the respect of intelligent persons and the affection of children;

To earn the approbation of honest critics,

And to endure the betrayal of false friends;

To appreciate beauty; to find the best in others;

To give one's self;

To leave the world a bit better, whether by a healthy child, a garden patch or a redeemed social condition;

To have played and laughed with enthusiasm and sung with exultation;

To know even one life has breathed easier because you have lived.

This is to have succeeded.

RALPH WALDO EMERSON

To be successful the first thing to do is fall in love with your work.

SISTER MARY LAURETTA

Satisfaction lies in the effort, not the attainment.
Full effort is full victory.

MAHATMA GANDHI

Being open means being free to do whatever is called for in a given situation. Because you do not want anything from the situation, you are free to act in the way genuinely appropriate to it. And similarly, if other people want something from you, that may be their problem. You do not have to try to ingratiate yourself with anyone. If you are comfortable being yourself, then an environment of openness and communication arises automatically and naturally. Situations develop automatically. We do not need to fit ourselves into special roles and environments.

CHÖGYAM TRUNGPA RINPOCHE

Take time to work—it is the price of success.

Take time to think—it is the source of power.

Take time to play—it is the secret of youth.

Take time to read—it is the foundation of knowledge.

Take time to worship—it is the highway of reverence and washes the dust of the earth from our eyes.

Take time to help and enjoy friends—it is the source of happiness.

Take time to love—it is the sacrament of life.

Take time to dream—it hitches the soul to the stars.

Take time to laugh—it is the singing that helps with life's load.

Take time for beauty—it is everywhere in nature.

Take time for health—it is the true wealth and treasure of life.

Take time to plan—it is the secret of being able to have time to take for the first eleven things!

How wonderful it is that nobody need wait a single moment before starting to improve the world.

ANNE FRANK

Since spiritual companions, couples, and so forth might be split up unexpectedly any moment, we had better avoid anger and quarrels, harsh words and fighting. We never know how long we might be together, so we should make up our minds to be caring and affectionate for the short while we have left. Remind yourself over and over again to treat everyone with respect and compassion.

PATRUL RINPOCHE

Satisfaction lies in the effort, not the attainment.
Full effort is full victory.

MAHATMA GANDHI

More things are wrought by prayer than this world dreams of.

ALFRED, LORD TENNYSON

For everyone who asks receives, and everyone who searches finds, and for everyone who knocks, the door will be open.

MATTHEW 7:7-8

The Buddha, the completely omniscient one, said that all phenomena are empty and devoid of self-entity. Normally, however, we perceive everything to be concrete and possessing individual identity.

CHÖKYI NYIMA RINPOCHE

Patient forbearance is the quality which enables us to prevent negative thoughts and emotions from taking hold of us. It safeguards our peace of mind in the face of adversity.

HIS HOLINESS THE 14TH DALAI LAMA

If a child is to keep alive his inborn sense of wonder without any such gifts from the fairies, he needs the companionship of at least one adult who can share it, rediscovering with him the joy, excitement, and mystery of the world we live in.

WILLIAM BLAKE

Patience is the companion of wisdom.

ST. AUGUSTINE OF HIPPO

Learn to be happy, here and now, under all conditions;
and to include others' happiness in your own joy.
Go out of your way to make others happy.

PARAMAHANSA YOGANANDA

Even if a bodhisattva, or a person who has realized that everything is an illusion, were to become a householder, he would have no need to be concerned with negative emotions or ego-clinging. He would be like a magician who knows very well the illusions he has created and, therefore, cannot be fooled by them. Understanding the void nature of worldly affairs, he would not be attracted to them or be afraid of them; he would have neither hope nor success nor fear of failure. Having confidence in his study, contemplation, and practice of the dharma, he would simply come closer and closer to the complete liberation.

DILGO KHYENTSE RINPOCHE

There is nothing that does not grow easier through
  habit.
Putting up with little troubles will prepare me to
  endure much sorrow.

SHANTIDEVA

A habit is the result of the concentration of the mind.

You have been thinking a certain way.

To form a new and good habit,

just concentrate in the opposite direction.

PARAMAHANSA YOGANANDA

When we come into contact with the other person, our thoughts and actions should express our mind of compassion, even if that person says and does things that are not easy to accept. We practice in this way until we see clearly that our love is not contingent upon the other person being lovable.

THICH NHAT HANH

It is God's play of light and shadow that
makes the world appear as it does to us.
When you realize this, you see
it as a dream motion picture.

PARAMAHANSA YOGANANDA

When you have truly attained the realization of this emptiness, you will be like the venerable Milarepa or Guru Rinpoche, who were unaffected by the heat of summer or the cold of winter, and who could not be burned by fire or drowned in water. In emptiness, there is neither pain nor suffering. We, on the other hand, have not understood the empty nature of the mind and so, when bitten by even a small insect, we think, "Ouch! I've been bitten. It hurts!" or when someone says something unkind, we get angry. That is the sign that we have not realized the mind's empty nature.

DILGO KHYENTSE RINPOCHE

If you add a little to a little, and then do it again, soon that little shall be much.

HESIOD

The soul is not permanently attached to its present
bodily and world environment, sex, or race,
but is omnipresent, eternal, free of any limitation.

PARAMAHANSA YOGANANDA

It is the enemy who can truly teach us to practice the virtues of compassion and tolerance.

HIS HOLINESS THE 14TH DALAI LAMA

To be spiritual is to be broad, to understand,
and to be a friend to all.

PARAMAHANSA YOGANANDA

As we begin to meditate more, we realize that the human mind is a wonderful thing. We are not trying to transcend the human mind in order to understand something more profound. All possible profundity is already within the mind. Generally speaking, if we look at how much of our mind we are using, we realize we are not using much. If we examine how deep and penetrating our experience is, we find it is very shallow, we could go a lot deeper. The point is that when we talk about experiencing things in a more profound way, we have to realize that those possibilities are within our basic human nature already.

SAKYONG MIPHAM RINPOCHE

Have patience with all things, but chiefly have patience with yourself. Do not lose courage in considering your own imperfections, but instantly set about remedying them—every day begin the task anew.

ST. FRANCIS DE SALES

No more evil action exists than one done out of hatred, and no merit is more difficult to practice than patient endurance. Try to quench the great fire of anger in your effort to attain patient endurance.

LONGCHENPA

Every saint who has penetrated the core of Reality has testified that a divine universal plan exists and that it is beautiful and full of joy.

PARAMAHANSA YOGANANDA

156

Speak few words, but say them with quietude and sincerity and they will be long-lasting.

LAO TZU

Love truth, and pardon error.

VOLTAIRE

A truth that's told with bad intent,
Beats all the lies you can invent.

WILLIAM BLAKE

Always be calm, like the pendulum that is still, but ready to swing into action whenever necessary.

PARAMAHANSA YOGANANDA

You have all the willpower in the world to break any habit. The power of divine will is always with you, and can never be destroyed.

PARAMAHANSA YOGANANDA

161

It is under the greatest adversity that there exists the greatest potential for doing good, both for oneself and others.

HIS HOLINESS THE 14TH DALAI LAMA

Don't be a mental fossil; be a living tree,
constantly spreading out new growth.
The strong-hearted soul says,
"There is sunshine in my life,
and I have every chance to throw out shoots
and branches of accomplishment."

PARAMAHANSA YOGANANDA

Fall seven times, stand up eight.

JAPANESE PROVERB

Open the door of your calmness
and let the footsteps of silence
gently enter the temple of all your activities.

PARAMAHANSA YOGANANDA

I am only one
But still I am one.
I cannot do everything,
But I can still do something.

EDWARD EVERETT HALE

Have balanced understanding.
If your understanding is governed
by both heart and head,
then you have clear vision to see yourself and others.

PARAMAHANSA YOGANANDA

To greet the day with reverence for the opportunities it contains; to hold ever before me, even in the doing of little things, the ultimate purpose to which I am working . . . this is how I desire to waste wisely my days.

THOMAS DEKKER

Mental whispers develop dynamic powers
to reshape matter into what you want.
Whatever you intensely believe in your mind
will materialize.

PARAMAHANSA YOGANANDA

From this moment until I obtain
the highest enlightenment,
I shall not permit ill-will or anger,
avarice or envy to occupy my mind.

ATISA

Where there is understanding, peace reigns.

PARAMAHANSA YOGANANDA

Is there any one maxim that ought to be acted upon throughout one's whole life? Surely the maxim of loving kindness is such.

CONFUCIUS

You are immortal and are endowed with eternal joy. Never forget this during your play with changeable mortal life.

PARAMAHANSA YOGANANDA

You can accomplish by kindness
what you cannot by force.

PUBLILIUS SYRUS

Learn to be happy, here and now, under all conditions;
and to include others' happiness in your own joy.
Go out of your way to make others happy.

PARAMAHANSA YOGANANDA

Always be kind, for everyone is fighting a hard battle.

PLATO

The focusing power of attention never fails.
It is the secret of success. Concentrate.
Then go after what you want.

PARAMAHANSA YOGANANDA

The best portion of a good man's life—
his little, nameless, unremembered acts
of kindness and love.

WILLIAM WORDSWORTH

Live uprightly and express your goodwill to all.
That is real morality.

PARAMAHANSA YOGANANDA

Compassion and love are not mere luxuries…
They are fundamental to the continued survival of
our species.

HIS HOLINESS THE 14TH DALAI LAMA

No matter what you are doing, keep the undercurrent of happiness, the secret river of joy, flowing beneath the sands of your various thoughts and the rocky soil of your hard trials. Learn to be secretly happy within your heart in spite of all circumstances.

PARAMAHANSA YOGANANDA

My religion is very simple. My religion is kindness.

HIS HOLINESS THE 14TH DALAI LAMA

Kindness is the light that dissolves all walls between souls, families, and nations.

PARAMAHANSA YOGANANDA

If a man's mind is concentrated and calm,
and if he has abandoned both good and evil,
there is no fear for him.

THE DHAMMAPADA

Have more mental strength. Develop such mental power that you can stand unshaken, no matter what comes, bravely facing anything in life.

PARAMAHANSA YOGANANDA

Hatred does not cease by hatred;
hatred ceases only by love.
This is the eternal law.

THE DHAMMAPADA

Profound sutras say that enlightenment is seeing the unseen itself, and in it there is no seeing and no seer— it is beginningless and endless calm.

ATISA

The material and the spiritual are but two parts of one universe and one truth.

PARAMAHANSA YOGANANDA

We really have to understand the person we want to love. If our love is only a will to possess, it is not love. If we only think of ourselves, know our own needs and ignore the needs of the other person, we cannot love.

THICH NHAT HANH

Come what may, then,
I will never harm my cheerful happiness of mind.
Depression never brings me what I want;
my virtue will be warped and marred by it.

SHANTIDEVA

As for View, Meditation, Action, and their Fruit:

Make freedom from aversion and attachment your
   View,

Make destruction of grasping intellectualization your
   Meditation,

Let freedom from craving and contrived deeds be your
   Conduct,

Let your Fruit be the abandonment of the wish to
   attain anything,

And thus realize the Dharmakaya which is
   spontaneously within!

DUDJOM RINPOCHE

Let nothing disturb you.
Let nothing frighten you.
Everything passes away except God.

ST. TERESA OF AVILA

Walking is meditation, sitting is meditation. Whether talking or remaining silent, whether moving or standing quiet, the essence itself is ever at ease; even when greeted with swords and spears, it never loses its quiet way, and all that befalls cannot perturb its serenity.

YOKA DAISHI

Learn to be happy, here and now, under all conditions;
and to include others' happiness in your own joy.
Go out of your way to make others happy.

PARAMAHANSA YOGANANDA

What wise man is eaten up with doubts about
happiness in his life and next?
Intelligent men make meditation the essential thing.

ATISA

My own mind is Buddha, but I never realize this.
Discursive thoughts are Dharmakaya
(ultimate reality),
but I don't realize this.
This is the unfabricated, innate natural state,
but I cannot keep to this.
Naturalness is things as they really are,
but I have no conviction in this.
Guru, think of me;
gaze quickly upon me with compassion.

                              JAMGON KONGTRUL

There is no more liberating action than sincerely to give people kindness in return for unkindness. Why not be like a flower that gives fragrance even when it is crushed in the hand?

PARAMAHANSA YOGANANDA

One master described meditation as "mind, suspended in space, nowhere."

SOGYAL RINPOCHE

In deep meditation the flow of concentration is continuous, like the flow of oil.

PATANJALI

Stop talking and thinking, then there is nowhere
you cannot go. Returning to the source, you gain the
meaning; chasing forms, you lose the wholeness.
A moment's true insight transcends all.

SOSAN

Learning to meditate is the greatest gift you can give
yourself in this life.

SOGYAL RINPOCHE

Hearing or reading the biographies of illumined
spiritual masters teaches us their wisdom and
enlightened way of life.

Simply to hear of the lives of such living Buddhas can
bring one onto the path of liberation.

DILGO KHYENTSE RINPOCHE

The ancient Indian master Shantideva states:
"Tigers, Lions, elephants, bears, snakes, all enemies,
guardians of hells and demons become controlled
by the mind alone. By subduing the mind alone, you
subdue them all." Once you have overcome your
demons, they can become helpers and guardians to
your meditation: their appearance is a normal part
of practice, but they will eventually pass away.
To meditate, let your mind rest in its natural
unrestrained and free state. By neither placing your
mind on something outside nor concentrating
inwardly, remain free of focus. Let your mind stay
unmoved, just like the flame of a butter lamp that is
not moved by the wind.

PADMASAMBHAVA

Just still the thoughts in your mind. It is good to do this right in the midst of disturbance.

YUANWU

One instant of total awareness is one of perfect freedom and enlightenment.

THE WISDOM DEITY, MANJUSHRI

The conflict of longing and loathing—
this is the disease of the heart.

SOSAN

When I teach meditation, I often begin by saying:
Bring your mind home. And release. And relax.

SOGYAL RINPOCHE

Suppose the loveliest of the land was dancing and singing and a crowd assembled. A man was there wishing to live, not to die, wishing for happiness, adverse to suffering. If someone said to him, "Good man, carry around this bowl of oil filled to the brim between the crowd and the girl. A man with a sword will follow you, and if you spill even a drop, he will cut off your head," would that man stop attending to that bowl of oil and turn his attention outward to the girl? This simile shows how you should train yourselves to direct awareness of the body.

THE BUDDHA

Let your awareness become heightened:
Let it spread out into the infinite sky.
From that state of complete openness,
That vast expanse, sing out!

LAMA SHABKAR

I go among trees and sit still. All my stirring becomes quiet around me like circles on water. My tasks lie in their places where I left them, asleep like cattle. Then what I am afraid of comes. I live for a while in its sight. What I fear in it leaves it. And the fear of it leaves me. It sings, and I hear its song.

WENDELL BERRY

What should we "do" with the mind in meditation?
Nothing. Just leave it, simply, as it is.

SOGYAL RINPOCHE

If the inner mind has been tamed, the outer enemy cannot harm you.

ATISA

When the empty looks at the empty, who is there to
look at something empty?

NYOSHUL KHENPO RINPOCHE

A meditation technique used in Tibetan Buddhism is uniting the mind with the sound of a mantra. The definition of mantra is "that which protects the mind."

SOGYAL RINPOCHE

What a lightning flash in the gloom it is for the self, cloaked in the darkness of ignorance, when awareness is gained even a little bit!

ATISA

Don't accept the pleasant or reject the awful, don't affirm or deny, but remain vividly awake in the state of unfabricated naturalness! By remaining like this, the sign of progress is that your body, speech, and mind feel free and easy, beyond pleasure and pain.

GURU PADMASAMBHAVA

Without asking about past or future, here and now,
just look! What is this? What truly is this
'I' who asks? Who sees, hears, feels and knows?
Who walks, stands, sits and lies down?
Or moves about restlessly? At all times, in all places,
look with all your heart and do not give
up looking for one moment. For this kind of looking,
neither reasons nor explanations are needed.
Just wholeheartedly look.
Thus you smash the ball of doubt.

MASTER DAIBI

Everything is found within the natural state, so do not seek elsewhere.

PADAMPA SANGYE

As pure awareness is the real Buddha, in openness and contentment I found the lama in my heart. When we realize that this unending natural mind is the very nature of the lama, then there is no need for attached, grasping or weeping prayers or complaints.

DUDJOM RINPOCHE

A hundred things may be explained to you, a thousand things told, but one thing only should you grasp. Know one thing and everything is freed— remain within your inner nature, your awareness.

GURU PADMASAMBHAVA

Do not build up your views upon your senses and thoughts, but at the same time do not seek the mind away from your senses and thoughts. When you are neither attached to nor detached from them, then you enjoy perfect unobstructed freedom, then you have the seat of enlightenment.

HUANG-PO HIS-YUAN

The spiritual man is not dependent upon externals. When there is nothing to screen oneself from outside views, one comes to oneself. This is where we stand free from distinctions and discriminations.

D.T. SUZUKI

When I dissolve into the vast expanse—empty and clear—without end, without limits— there is no difference between mind and sky.

LAMA SHABKAR

When you are inspired by some great purpose,
all your thoughts break their bonds. Your mind
transcends limitations, your consciousness expands in
every direction and you find yourself in a new, great,
and wonderful world. Dormant forces, faculties, and
talents become alive, and you discover yourself to be a
greater person by far than you ever dreamed
yourself to be.

PATANJALI

Let it be, open and bright like the sky,

without taking sides,

with no clouds of concepts.

LONGCHENPA

What life can compare with this? Sitting quietly by
the window, I watch leaves fall and the flowers bloom
as the seasons come and go.

SECCHO

I attribute my sense of peace to the effort to develop concern for others.

HIS HOLINESS THE 14TH DALAI LAMA

229

Through the internal way of profound HUNG recitation, clinging to appearances is stopped and the power of awareness increases.

GURU PADMASAMBHAVA

He who lives in harmony with himself lives in harmony with the world.

MARCUS AURELIUS

Not thinking about anything is Zen. Once you know this, walking, standing, sitting or lying down, everything you do is Zen.

To know that the mind is empty is to see the Buddha. Using the mind to look for reality is delusion. Not using the mind to look for reality is awareness. Freeing yourself from words is liberation.

BODHIDHARMA

Do not think about the thinkable. Do not think about the unthinkable. By thinking about neither the thinkable nor the unthinkable, you will see voidness.

GAMPOPA

Fidelity to grace in my life is fidelity to simplicity,
rejecting ambition and analysis and elaborate thought,
or even elaborate concern. A breath of Zen blows all
these cobwebs out the window.

THOMAS MERTON

The Himalayas with their high snow peaks are
  dancing,
Joining rhythm in the dance, joining with the stillness,
The most dignified movement of them all.

CHÖGYAM TRUNGPA RINPOCHE

These are our actors,
As I foretold you were all spirits and
Are melted into air, into air:
... And, like this insubstantial pageant faded,
Leave not a rack behind: We are such stuff
As dreams are made on, and our little life
Is rounded with a sleep.

WILLIAM SHAKESPEARE

Act without acting on.

Work without working at.

LAO TZU

The arising of realization is like the dispelling of darkness by the sun.

LONGCHEN RABJAM

Three things in human life are important.
The first is to be kind.
The second is to be kind.
And the third is to be kind.

HENRY JAMES

Compassion has been achieved when we have cast off
the shackles of cherishing ourself more than others
and there is a real, rather than verbal, longing that all
beings may be liberated from suffering.

GAMPOPA

Compassion is the wish-fulfilling gem, the auspicious jar from which the splendor of good fortune comes; it is the finest medicine from which happiness derives, because the disease of living beings is cured. It is the sun of pristine cognitions, the moon soothing afflictions. It is like the sky, studded with the stars of spotless qualities, always bringing about prosperity and bliss.

LONGCHENPA

Were our own mother to be tormented by hunger and thirst, full of fear, completely disheartened, would we not feel very much compassion for her? Those deprived spirits who suffer torments like these have all been our own mothers. How can we not feel compassion?

GAMPOPA

Unobscured by clouds or darkness, the sun shines in the sky by its very nature.

LONGCHENPA

I would rather feel compassion than know the meaning of it.

ST. THOMAS AQUINAS

It is important not to allow ourselves to be put off by the magnitude of others' suffering. The misery of millions is not a cause for pity. Rather it is a cause for compassion.

HIS HOLINESS THE 14TH DALAI LAMA

Bravery is stability, not of legs and arms, but of courage and the soul.

MICHEL DE MONTAIGNE

When sitting, sit; when standing, stand.
Above all, don't wobble.

ZEN SAYING

Don't invite the future.
Don't pursue the past.
Let go of the present.
Relax, right now.

GAMPOPA

Wheresoever you go, go with all your heart.

CONFUCIUS

Whatever I have tried to do in life,
I have tried with all my heart to do it well.

CHARLES DICKENS

If there is a cure when trouble comes, what need is there for being sad? And if no cure is to be found, what use is there in sorrow?

SHANTIDEVA

Grief can be the garden of compassion. If you keep your heart open through everything, your pain can become your greatest ally in your life's search for love and wisdom.

JALAL UD-DIN RUMI

Impermanence is suffering.

All beings are impermanent and die.

Haven't you heard about the people who died in the past? Haven't you seen any of your relatives die? Don't you notice that we grow old?

And still rather than practicing the Dharma, you forget about past grief.

GURU PADMASAMBHAVA

In meditation, be free of clinging to experiences.

PADAMPA SANGYE

Have patience and endure:
this unhappiness will one day be beneficial.

OVID

It requires more courage to suffer than to die.

NAPOLEAN BONAPARTE

When a particular perception, perverted or not, occurs frequently, it grows stronger and grips our mind. Then it becomes difficult to get rid of that perception.

PIYADASSI THERA

This world of appearance has, from the very beginning, never come into existence and is like a mirror image. It has no substance, yet it appears to be there. Having seen this, you quickly reach the citadel of sublime nonattachment.

LONGCHENPA

Buddha is a scientist of the inner world. Meditation is his basic contribution—turning the horizontal consciousness into a vertical consciousness.

OSHO

Developing a true sense of gratitude involves taking absolutely nothing for granted. Rather, we always look for the friendly intention behind the deed and learn to appreciate it.

ALBERT SCHWEITZER

What is, is not; what is not, is.

Unless you truly have understood this,

you must not tarry in what seems.

One in all, all in one.

SOSAN

Gratitude is not only the greatest of virtues, but the parent of all the others.

CICERO

The fundamental delusion of humanity is to suppose
that I am here and you are out there.

YASUTANI ROSHI

To walk the Middle Way is to say a big "yes" to life, to the good as well as the bad, to good fortune as well as ill. It is to walk right down the middle, facing up to suffering and all, without avoiding anything that life brings or being carried away by success or failure, praise or blame, suffering or pleasure.

THE MIDDLE WAY
(JOURNAL OF THE BUDDHIST SOCIETY)

Men in general judge more from appearances than from reality. All men have eyes, but few have the gift of penetration.

NICCOLO MACHIAVELLI

Those who have the smallest grain of wisdom would want to walk the simple path of the Great Way. Their only fear would be to go astray.

LAO TZU

Stop attachments, coveting, desires, and let go of embarrassment and timidity in doing deeds that increase merit and engage your talent.

SHANTIDEVA

We are what we think.

All that we are arises with our thoughts.

With our thoughts we make the world.

Speak or act with an impure mind and trouble will
follow you

As the wheel follows the ox that draws the cart.

We are what we think.

All that we are arises with our thoughts. With our
thoughts we made the world.

Speak or act with a pure mind and happiness will
follow you

As your shadow unshakeable.

THE DHAMMAPADA

I gave up sewn clothes and wore a robe, but I noticed one day the cloth was well-woven. So I bought some burlap, but I still throw it elegantly over my shoulder. I pulled back my sensual longings and now I discover I'm angry a lot. I gave up rage, and now I notice that I'm greedy all day. I worked hard at dissolving the greed, and now I'm proud of myself. When the mind wants to break its link with the world, it still holds on to one thing.

KABIR

Although this body that is the foundation of all frustrations and unhappiness and the great birthplace of the emotions may be decked with clothes, jewelry and flower garlands, or be pleased and gratified with delicious food and drink, finally you have to part with it because it is transitory and fragile.

LONGCHENPA

Fire may become cold, the wind may be caught
by a rope, sun and moon may fall down, but the
consequence of karma is infallible.

GAMPOPA

Cling not to memories or experiences: they are ever changing.

PADAMPA SANGYE

Bodhi [enlightenment] is to be looked for in your own
  mind.
You seek in vain for a solution to the mystery in the
  outside world.

MATSUO BASHŌ

In Tibetan, the word for "body" is lu, which means "something you leave behind," like baggage. Each time we say lu, it reminds us that we are only travelers, taking temporary refuge in this life and body.

SOGYAL RINPOCHE

If the heart is in accord with what is, all single strivings have ceased, all doubts are cleared up, true faith is confirmed; nothing remains, nothing need be remembered. Empty, clear, self-illuminating, the heart does not waste its energy.

SOSAN

Happiness is not something ready-made. It comes from your own actions.

HIS HOLINESS THE 14TH DALAI LAMA

The cycle of rebirth springs from conceptual thought, which is its very nature. The complete removal of such thought is the highest nirvana.

ATISA

If others are happy, the great sages rejoice. If others are sad, the sages are sad. When others are content, all the sages rejoice.

ATISA

There is a light that shines beyond all things on Earth, beyond us all, beyond the highest, the very highest heavens. This is the light that shines in our heart.

THE UPANISHADS

Just as cotton is swayed in the direction of the wind's coming and going, so should we surrender ourselves to our enthusiasm, and in this way our powers will thrive.

SHANTIDEVA

...To see the world in a grain of sand,

And a heaven in a wild flower,

Hold infinity in the palm of your hand

And eternity in an hour.

WILLIAM BLAKE

I think that all happiness depends on the energy to assume the mask of some other self; that all joyous or creative life is a rebirth as something not oneself.

W. B. YEATS

After all, it is no more surprising to be born twice than it is to be born once.

VOLTAIRE

Life is very short and many are the kinds of knowledge; let him who knows not even his own life's span choose only from his purest desires.

ATISA

One joy scatters a hundred griefs.

CHINESE PROVERB

ho believe in physics, know that the

een past, present, and future is only a

stent illusion.

ALBERT EINSTEIN

If an Arab in the desert were suddenly to discover a spring in his tent, and so would always be able to have water in abundance, how fortunate he would consider himself—so too when a man, who as a physical being is always turned towards the outside, thinking that his happiness lies outside him, finally turns inward and discovers that the source is within.

SOREN KIERKEGAARD

A person's life is passing with every minute or second; day and night it moves closer to the domain of the Lord of Death, just like the water of a waterfall flowing into the ocean, or the sun setting behind the mountain.

LONGCHENPA

If you . . . follow your bliss, you put yourself on a kind of track that has been there all the while, waiting for you, and the life that you ought to be living is the one you are living.

JOSEPH CAMPBELL

Laziness may appear attractive,
but work gives satisfaction.

ANNE FRANK

Do not become conceited just because you happen to be somewhat quick and clever; the clever ones need all the more to rely on their heart's aspiration. And if you deem yourself stupid and dull, unable to keep up with most people, rely still more upon this aspiration of the heart. Never be content with small attainment but still more rely on this aspiration in the heart.

TOREI ENJI ZENJI

For everything there is a season, and a time for every matter under heaven.

ECCLESIASTES 3:1

A man may fulfil the object of his existence by asking a question he cannot answer, and attempting a task he cannot achieve.

OLIVER WENDELL HOLMES

We cling to our own point of view as though
everything depended on it.
Yet our opinions have no permanence:
like autumn and winter, they gradually pass away.

CHUANG TZU

As this life, like a lamp in the wind,

has little certainty of lasting,

we must begin in earnest to keep meditation

like a flame burning in

the head or body.

ATISA

Learning doesn't just mean to receive teachings;
it means to cut through misconceptions and have
realizations beyond conceptual mind.

GURU PADMASAMBHAVA

Out, out, brief candle!

Life is but a walking shadow, a poor player...

WILLIAM SHAKESPEARE

All truths are easy to understand once they are discovered; the point is to discover them.

GALILEO GALILEI

All things change; nothing perishes.

OVID

299

Rely on the message of the teacher, not his personality; rely on the meaning, not just the words; rely on the real meaning, not the provisional one; rely on your wisdom mind, not your ordinary, judgmental mind.

THE BUDDHA

The world of life and death is created by mind, is in bondage to mind, is ruled by mind; and the mind is master to every situation. As the wheel follows the ox that pulls the cart, suffering follows the mind that surrounds itself with impure thoughts and worldly possessions.

THE LANKAVATARA SUTRA

In my tradition we revere the masters for being even kinder than the Buddhas themselves.

We cannot meet the Buddhas face to face.

But we can meet the masters; they are here, living, breathing, speaking, and acting to show us the way to liberation.

SOGYAL RINPOCHE

As the same person inhabits the body through childhood, youth, and old age, so too at the time of death he attains another body. The wise are not deluded by these changes.

THE BHAGAVAD GITA

The spirit and the body carry different loads and require different attentions. Too often we put the saddlebags on Jesus and let the donkey run loose.

JALAL UD-DIN RUMI

If you chase wildly around, wanting to follow others, even after thousands of years you will only end up by returning to birth and death. Better it is . . . crossing one's legs on the mediation cushion, to just sit.

RINZAI

Two monks were watching a flag blow in the wind.

One monk said, "The flag is moving."

The other monk said, "No, the wind is moving."

A Zen master happened to be passing by,

and he told them,

"Not the wind, nor flag; the mind is moving."

ZEN STORY

When a Buddhist offers flowers or lights a lamp before the Buddha image or some sacred object . . . these are not acts of worship. The flowers soon fade, and the flames that die down speak to him, and tell him of the impermanency of all things.

PIYADASSI THERA

The man who can repeat but little of the teaching but lives it himself, who forsakes craving, hatred and delusion, clings to nothing in this or any other world—he is a follower of the Blessed One.

THE DHAMMAPADA

In nature there are neither rewards nor punishments—
there are consequences.

ROBERT GREEN INGERSOLL

There is no need for temples, no need for complicated philosophies. My brain and my heart are my temples; my philosophy is kindness.

HIS HOLINESS THE 14TH DALAI LAMA

When you say the first syllable, Om, it is blessed
to help you achieve perfection in the practice of
generosity, Ma helps the practice of pure ethics, and
Ni helps the practice of tolerance and patience. Pad,
the fourth syllable, helps perseverance, Me helps
concentration, and the sixth syllable, Hum, helps the
practice of wisdom.

GEN RINPOCHE

In the case of such global issues as the conservation of the Earth, and indeed in taking all problems, the human mind is the key factor. Though these issues seem to go beyond anyone's individual capacity, where the problem begins and where the answer must be first sought is within. In order to change the external situation we must first change within ourselves. If we want a beautiful garden, we must first have a blueprint in the imagination, a vision. Then that idea can be implemented and the external garden can be materialized.

HIS HOLINESS THE 14TH DALAI LAMA

Prayer is not asking. It is a language of the soul.

MAHATMA GANDHI

There are many instances where people have gained
enlightenment by merely watching a leaf fall,
the flow of water, a forest fire, the blowing out
of a lamp.

PIYADASSI THERA

He prayeth best, who loveth best
All things both great and small.

SAMUEL TAYLOR COLERIDGE

The smallest amount of merit dedicated to the good of others is more precious than any amount of merit devoted to our own good.

GAMPOPA

When my house burned down

I gained an unobstructed view of the moonlit sky.

(renunciation/letting go)

ZEN

But pleasures are like poppies spread,
You seize the flower, its bloom is shed,
Or like the snow falls on a river,
A moment white—then melts forever.

ROBERT BURNS

In the hope of reaching the moon, men fail to see the flowers that bloom beneath their feet.

ALBERT SCHWEITZER

Humankind has not woven the web of life.

We are but one thread within it.

Whatever we do to the web, we do to ourselves.

All things are bound together.

CHIEF SEATTLE

Do you want long life and happiness?
Seek peace, and pursue it with all your heart.

PSALMS 34:12, 14

Hurtful expressions should never be used, not even against an enemy, for inevitably they will return to us, like an echo from a rock.

GAMPOPA

Peace, in the sense of the absence of war, is of little value to someone who is dying of hunger or cold. It will not remove the pain of torture.
Peace can only last where human rights are respected, where people are fed and where individuals and nations are free.

HIS HOLINESS THE 14TH DALAI LAMA

Support living beings with your whole nature and protect them like your own body.

NAGAJUNA

All know the way;
few actually walk it.

BODHIDHARMA

There never was a good war or a bad peace.

BENJAMIN FRANKLIN

All things depend on something else.
Thus, when enemies or friends are seen to act
improperly, be serene and tell yourself,
"This is because of such and such."

SHANTIDEVA

We look forward to a time when the power of love will replace the love of power. Then will our world know the blessings of peace.

WILLIAM GOLDSTONE

He who wishes to secure the goods of others, has already secured his own.

CONFUCIUS

Without inner peace, it is impossible to have world peace.

HIS HOLINESS THE 14TH DALAI LAMA

Everything that irritates us about others can lead us to an understanding of ourselves.

CARL JUNG

I heartily accept the motto,
"That government which is best which governs the least," and I should like to see acted upon more rapidly and systematically. Carried out, it finally amounts to this, which I also believe, "That government is best which governs not at all," and when men are prepared for it, that will be the kind of government which they will have.

HENRY DAVID THOREAU

If you master others, you are forceful.
If you master yourself, you have
inner strength.

LAO TZU

Dharma is good, but what constitutes Dharma?
Little evil, much good, kindness, generosity,
truthfulness, and purity.

ASHOKA

Your life is the fruit of your own doing.
You have no one to blame but yourself.

JOSEPH CAMPBELL

When it shall be said, in any country in the world, my people are happy; my jails are empty;
the aged are not in want, the taxes are not oppressive . . . then may that country boast of its constitution and its government.

THOMAS PAINE

In the cycle of existence that has neither beginning
nor end, even my enemy has been my father
or mother and has added to my prosperity.
Can I offer malice to repay kindness?

LONGCHENPA

Love and compassion are necessities, not luxuries.
Without them, humanity cannot survive.

HIS HOLINESS THE 14TH DALAI LAMA

Where there is charity and wisdom,
there is neither fear nor ignorance.

ST. FRANCIS OF ASSISI

Nobody can hurt me without my permission.

MAHATMA GANDHI

No act of kindness, however small, is ever wasted.

AESOP

Answer with kindness when faced with hostility.

LAO TZU

Though I have the gift of prophecy and understand all mysteries; though I have all faith, so that I could move mountains, and have not charity, I am nothing.

1 CORINTHIANS 13:2

Whenever someone has offended me, I try to raise my soul so high that the offence cannot reach it.

RENÉ DESCARTES

The life of a man consists not in seeing visions and dreaming dreams, but in active charity and in willing service.

HENRY WADSWORTH LONGFELLOW

Just as a bird with unfledged wings cannot fly up into the sky, so, without the power of wisdom, we cannot work for the good of others.

ATISA

345

The mind, imbued with love and compassion in thought and deed, ought ever to be directed to the service of all sentient beings.

GAMPOPA

Every time you breathe in, thank a tree.

JOHN WRIGHT

Knowledge should go hand in hand with purity of heart, with moral excellence.

PIYADASSI THERA

This above all—to thine own self be true.

WILLIAM SHAKESPEARE

Be content with simple things and free from the craving for worldly possessions.

GAMPOPA

Let nature be your teacher.

WILLIAM WORDSWORTH

When you come right down to it, the secret of having it all is loving it all.

DR. JOYCE BROTHERS

As men think, so they are, both here and hereafter, thoughts being the parent of all actions, good and bad. As the sowing has been, so will the harvest be.

THE TIBETAN BOOK OF THE DEAD

Karma is about choice.

We can go up or down, to the heavens or the hells.

We are arbiters of our own fate.

With the Buddha's help we can avoid these realms by
not creating any karma.

This is the Middle Path.

BRYAN APPLEYARD

A good man says no slowly;
a wise man says no at once.

KATRINA GRAHAM

Of all the excellent things there are in the world and beyond this world, intelligent men take meditation as the best.

ATISA

It was once said that the moral
test of a government is how that government treats
those who are in the dawn of life, the children; those
who are in the twilight of life, the elderly; and those
who are in the shadows
of life, the sick, the needy, and the
handicapped.

HUBERT H. HUMPHREY

A man's true wealth is the good that he does in this world to his fellows.

MUHAMMAD

Hampton Roads Publishing Company

. . . for the evolving human spirit

Hampton Roads Publishing Company publishes books on a
variety of subjects, including spirituality, health,
and other related topics.

For a copy of our latest catalog, call (978) 465-0504 or
visit our distributor's website at *www.redwheelweiser.com*.
You can also sign up for our newsletter and special offers by
going to *www.redwheelweiser.com/newsletter*.